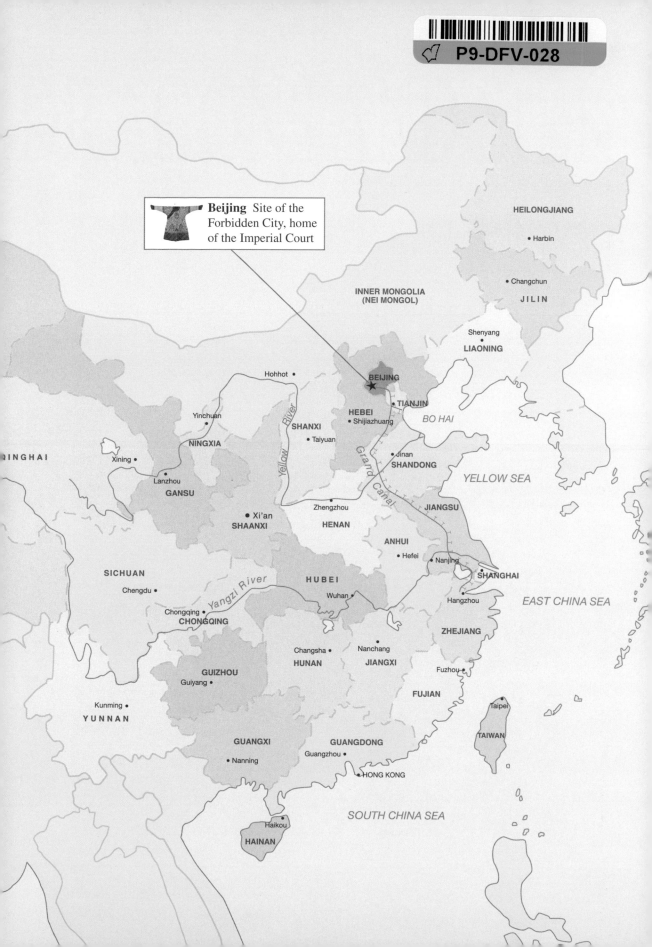

Mandarin in court attire,
gouache painting, 19th century

Mandarin's wife in court attire,
gouache painting, 19th century

DRAGONS AND SILK FROM THE FORBIDDEN CITY

 The art of Chinese embroidery predates painting in early China and has always been considered one of the highest art forms. Beauty and magic were associated with silk in early times. 'We . . . dressed ourselves like flowers in embroidered clothing,' recorded a shaman describing a ritual during the Han dynasty (206 BC–AD 220).

The production of silk extends back to 2000 BC, when Xiling Shi, the consort of the legendary Yellow Emperor, was said to have discovered how to make silk cloth from the silkworm cocoon. One of the earliest surviving pieces of evidence of silk weaving is a Shang dynasty (*c.* 1600–1027 BC) fragment, transmuted in the patina of two bronzes.

In ancient times silk was as precious as gold. The secret of its manufacture was not discovered in the West until the Middle Ages. Indeed it was for the purpose of acquiring China's fabulous silks that the trade routes between East and West were first opened.

Over 2,000 years of painstaking labour has left us with a collection of work that reflects the cosmic philosophies, the poetry and the power of China. Some of the finest embroideries were made for the Imperial Court in the Forbidden City, where the palace studio employed thousands of artisans to produce robes and hangings for the imperial family's personal use.

*Winter **jifu** of deep blue satin silk with nine gold couched dragons surrounded by auspicious emblems. Trimmed with fur. c. 1850.*

JIFU: FORMAL COURT DRAGON ROBE

The emperor, princes and mandarins wore these fine silk robes as emblems of their office. (Mandarins were civil and military officials, appointed through a strict and rigorous public examination process. Their advancement depended on merit.) The strict ceremonial laws of the Qing dynasty (1644–1911), established in 1759 and enforced in 1766, required that mandarins wore robes covered in dragons and other symbols for all formal and ceremonial occasions. These robes are known as *longpao* or dragon robes.

The ancient Chinese believed that dragons were benevolent creatures whose breath turned into clouds and whose power manifested itself in thunder and rain. The dragon also represented storms, good luck, virility, authority and the creative, dynamic force in the universe. From the Han dynasty (206 BC–AD 220) onwards, dragons were the symbol of the emperor. There are always nine dragons on the *jifu*, with the ninth hidden under the fold-over front; nine is an auspicious number denoting virility and power. The dragons are shown either holding or chasing the Flaming Pearl of Wisdom and Truth. This symbolizes the wearer's desire to attain inner wisdom.

The design represents a diagram of the universe, the combination of symbols having cosmic significance. At the hem of the robe is the *lishui* border, represented by diagonal stripes for water, and above that is the sea with its rolling waves. The Earth-Mountains are represented by four tall mountain peaks. The air element and clouds are above the mountains and the neck of the robe represents the Gate of Heaven. The symbolism is completed when the robe is worn, with the wearer's head representing Heaven.

Jifu of embroidered blue silk, the nine dragons couched in gold. This robe would have been made for a high-ranking mandarin, since it shows the lower dragons grasping the Flaming Pearl of Wisdom and Truth. c. 1870.

The court robes were designed, through the use of symbols, to reinforce the divine right of the emperor, who was regarded as a 'God on Earth'. Confucius (551–479 BC) once said of the emperor: 'Let his faculties and his virtues that are so powerful make him equal with Heaven.'

A mandarin wearing the dragon robe represented the authority of the emperor and carried the power to institute the will of the emperor and administer his laws and punishments.

*An embroidered brown satin silk jifu with nine gold couched dragons and ribbed
indigo silk sleeves embroidered with bats. There were five shades of yellow; brown,
being a 'lesser yellow', was worn by members of the imperial clan. c. 1770.*

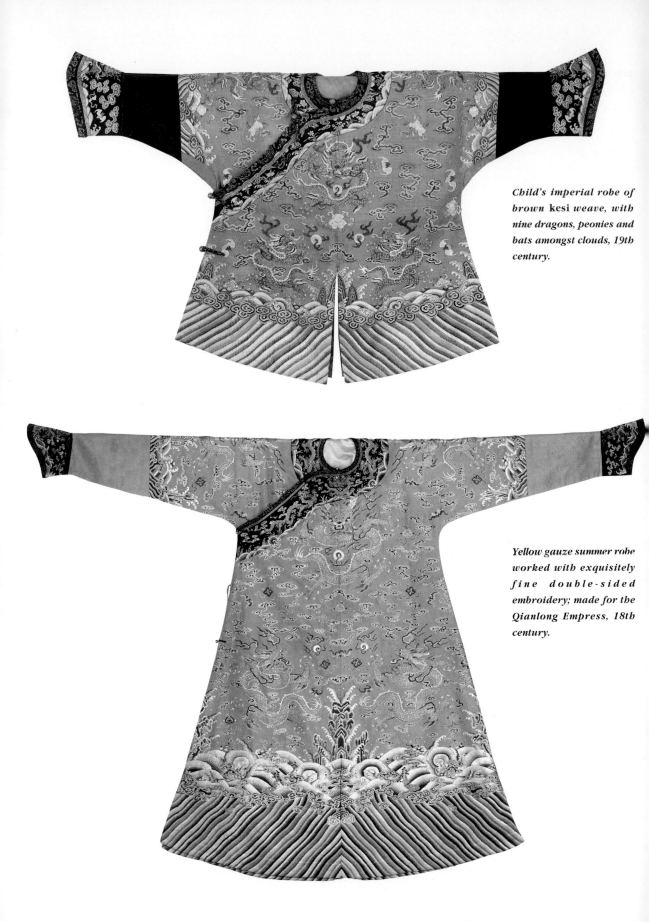

Child's imperial robe of brown kesi weave, with nine dragons, peonies and bats amongst clouds, 19th century.

Yellow gauze summer robe worked with exquisitely fine double-sided embroidery; made for the Qianlong Empress, 18th century.

Imperial Robes with the 12 Symbols of Authority

Confucius, in his *Analects*, describes the relationship between dress and *li* (righteousness):

> 'He (the emperor) adjusts his clothes and cap and throws a dignity into his looks, so that thus dignified, he is looked at in awe—is not this to be majestic without being fierce?'

The style of the emperor's *jifu* and that of the princes and mandarins who served him was the same. In 1759 a law was passed whereby the emperor's robe had to be distinguished by the inclusion of the 12 signs of imperial authority. The incorporation of these symbols completed the message that the emperor had a mandate from Heaven to rule over all creation. These symbols had been used by the Ming (1368–1644) and previous dynasties, but had not been adopted by the Qing until decreed in 1759.

The laws of the Qing dynasty also required the emperor and empress to wear yellow robes for all special occasions. Exceptions were made for the four great annual sacrifices, when a specific colour was demanded by the occasion. These robes were very rare, being worn only for the specific

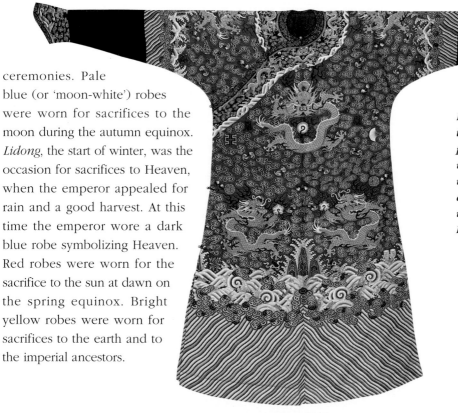

ceremonies. Pale blue (or 'moon-white') robes were worn for sacrifices to the moon during the autumn equinox. *Lidong*, the start of winter, was the occasion for sacrifices to Heaven, when the emperor appealed for rain and a good harvest. At this time the emperor wore a dark blue robe symbolizing Heaven. Red robes were worn for the sacrifice to the sun at dawn on the spring equinox. Bright yellow robes were worn for sacrifices to the earth and to the imperial ancestors.

For sacrificial ceremonies to the God of Grain or ritual prayers for rain, the emperor would have worn a blue robe with the 12 symbols of authority. This 12-symbol kesi woven robe was made for Emperor Tongzhi. c. 1870.

The 12 Symbols of Authority

The 12 symbols of authority were arranged in order of importance, in three rings falling at the neck, waist and knees.

 The Sun—Located on the left shoulder, the sun is represented by a three-legged bird in a yellow disc, symbolizing Heaven and intellectual enlightenment. The number three is the symbol of the masculine principle, of which the sun is the essence.

 The Moon—On the right shoulder is a white moon disc, within which the Hare of the Moon is pounding with a pestle to obtain the elixir of immortality.

 Constellation—Above the principal dragon on the chest is an arrangement of three small discs, representing stars in a constellation and symbolic of Heaven and the cosmic universe.

 Mountains—Located on the back, above the principal dragon, are mountains, signifying the earth.

The sun, moon, constellation and mountains represented the four annual sacrifices made by the emperor and together indicated his authority over the whole universe.

Pair of Dragons—These symbolize the emperor's adaptability through transformation or renewal.

 Pheasant—Exemplifies literary refinement and education.

 Fu—A character meaning discernment of good and evil or judgement.

 Axe—This denotes temporal power and justice in the punishment of crime.

 Water Weeds—The water weeds rise and fall with the seasons, representing responses to the needs of the moment.

 Libation Cups—A pair of bronze libation cups represent the element of metal and signify filial piety.

 Flames—Flames symbolize intellectual brilliance and zeal for virtue.

Grain—A plate of millet or grain denotes the emperor's responsibility to feed the people.

These 12 symbols completed the message that the emperor, the Son of Heaven, had control over all creation as regent for the Lord of Heaven.

Yellow embroidered jifu with the 12 symbols of authority, c. 1820,
made for Emperor Daoguang (reigned 1821–1851).

MAN'S *CHAOFU* : CEREMONIAL COURT DRAGON ROBE

The *chaofu* was the most formal costume at the imperial court during the Qing dynasty, being worn only 12 times a year at the principal sacrificial ceremonies conducted at dawn by the emperor himself. The torches held up high during the processions would have lit up the magnificent gold couched dragons, prominent against the deep indigo silk which merged with the darkness as the mandarins and princes accompanied the Son of Heaven to his annual sacrifices. Although it is the costume most frequently shown in Qing ancestor portraits, the *chaofu* is extremely rare, since only the most high-ranking mandarins were allowed to wear it.

The Ming dynasty was ruled by emperors from the Han majority, an agricultural and sedentary people based around the fertile valleys of the Yangtze and Yellow rivers of central China. The Ming dynasty garments were made with voluminous amounts of silk, as this was a mark of refinement and elegance. The people who ended Ming rule and established the Qing dynasty in 1644 were from Manchuria. These nomadic people from the cold steppes of north-central Asia were excellent and hardy equestrians. Their horses played a central role in their culture and they were able to ride long distances, hunting by bow and arrow. Their clothing, unlike that worn during the Ming dynasty, reflected the need for freedom of movement, as well as the demands of keeping warm while spending long hours in the saddle. Close-fitting tunics, with long cuffs that covered the hands resting on the pommel of the saddle, were features of the Manchu national costume.

Man's **chaofu,** *rare ceremonial court robe. c. 1870.*

These horseshoe-shape cuffs were cut to protect the backs of the hands, while still allowing the fingers to work the reins. Below the tunic, the Manchu warrior wore leggings covered by a pair of pleated aprons, open in the middle and back.

The cut of the *chaofu* was based on this traditional Manchu riding outfit, though modified somewhat for the more sedate demands of court and diplomacy. From the outset, the Manchus were determined to preserve their culture and heritage, so they made their national costumes a symbol of authority and rule. The traditional Han Chinese court attire was banned and the Manchu imposed their national costumes on all who attended court. Thus the Manchu conquerors kept a separate ethnic identity through the regulation of costume. As the rulers of Heaven and Earth, however, the Qing emperors were obliged to continue the rites and ceremonies required by the mandate of Heaven. For this reason, the Manchus continued to use ancient Chinese imperial symbolism to decorate their robes.

WOMAN'S *CHAOFU* : FORMAL COURT DRAGON ROBE

The woman's formal *chaofu* is the only court costume to be cut with inset sleeves. Like the man's *chaofu*, it was based on traditional Manchu costume. The woman's *chaofu* is rarer than the man's, as there were fewer occasions on which it could be worn.

Woman's **chaofu,** *rare ceremonial court robe. There were five shades of yellow, and brown, being a 'lesser yellow', was worn by members of the imperial clan. This robe would have been made for a princess or noblewoman. c. 1770.*

BUFU : MANDARIN'S SURCOAT

Mandarins wore a plain, front-opening surcoat over their robes. This was made of dark blue silk, decorated only by a square badge on the front and back. The badge indicated the wearer's office and rank, either civil or military. This surcoat *(bufu)* covered the entire dragon robe, with only the *lishui* wave border visible at the bottom and the horseshoe cuffs visible at the wrists. It seems strange that the sumptuously decorated dragon robes should have been entirely covered, but there was a reason for this. The Emperor Qianlong (reigned 1736–1795) wanted to remind his officials that the reason for wearing the dragon robe was not for outward pomp and circumstance, but rather for the inner spiritual power that the symbolism of the robe represented. It was Qianlong who passed the imperial edict specifying the code of dress to be worn at court. As with the *chaofu*, this simple coat was based on Manchu tradition.

Mandarin's surcoat, bufu, *with a rank badge insignia of a golden pheasant, which would have been worn by a second rank civil official.*

BUZI : RANK BADGES

The mandarin square, or rank badge, was an embroidered or woven square. It indicated which of the nine ranks of civil and military officials the wearer had attained. The official's wife always took on the rank of her husband and she would also wear a rank badge. Military officials wore badges showing an animal, while civil officials wore badges with a bird. The imperial family wore *bufu* with embroidered dragon roundels. The badge was either integrated onto the *bufu* during its manufacture or appliquéd, allowing the wearer to upgrade his rank without having to replace his coat. The practice of wearing these badges as official marks of rank first arose during the Yuan dynasty (1279–1368), was continued by the Ming and then adopted by the Qing.

Imperial rank badge with gourd and canopy, worn for the Lantern Festival and New Year. Late Ming dynasty, 17th century.

Civil officials had greater status than their military counterparts. It is believed that birds were chosen for the civil ranks because, having the ability to fly, they were regarded as being closer to Heaven and thus associated with literary talent and wisdom. By contrast, animals, although more physically powerful, were earthbound and considered less endowed in relation to knowledge. Each of the birds or animals is shown looking up towards a red sun, which authorities believe comes from the ancient proverb 'keep your eye on the sun and rise high'. The background is filled with clouds, bats, water, mountains and other auspicious symbols.

Civil Badges of Rank

First rank   Crane
Second rank   Golden pheasant
Third rank   Peacock
Fourth rank   Wild goose
Fifth rank   Silver pheasant
Sixth rank   Egret
Seventh rank   Mandarin duck
Eighth rank   Quail
Ninth rank   Paradise flycatcher

Early Qing dynasty rank badge showing a peacock, the insignia of a third rank civil official. Early Qing rank badges had fewer symbols and more open design than those of later rank badges. This rare example has a background of straight-laid gold couching, with couched peacock feather rock and satin stitch bird. c.1680.

Rank badge showing a silver pheasant, the insignia of a fifth rank civil official. The design is worked in fine Peking knot stitch on a ground entirely couched in gold-wrapped threads. c. 1850.

Kesi rank badge showing a goose, the insignia of a fourth rank civil official. The goose is surrounded by peonies, bats and clouds. c. 1880.

Rank badge with the paradise flycatcher, insignia of a civil official of the ninth rank, the design worked in fine Peking knot stitch on a ground entirely couched in gold-wrapped threads. c. 1850.

Kesi rank badge showing a mandarin duck, the insignia of a seventh rank civil official. In the surrounding sky are Taoist symbols, with Buddhist emblems floating in the waves. c. 1870.

MANGAO : INFORMAL DRAGON ROBE

The third style of dragon robe, the *mangao*, was worn for travelling and social gatherings when full formal attire was not required. For the Chinese red was the colour of joy and celebration. Red robes with auspicious symbols were worn at festivals like the lunar New Year, birthdays and weddings. A candidate who had just passed the imperial examinations would have worn a red robe with eight dragons. On her wedding day, a bride would wear a pleated silk skirt and a short red robe decorated with dragons (masculine) and phoenix (feminine), reflecting the dual nature of the universe. The phoenix was said to have five colours of feathers, after the five cardinal virtues, and its song had five notes that resembled the music of pan pipes. This mythical bird represents *yin* (feminine energy), goodness and prosperity and became associated with the empress. The phoenix's appearance on the bridal gown indicated that the bride was 'empress for the day'.

This kesi mangao, *decorated with cranes (symbols of longevity), was probably made to be worn at a wedding or anniversary. Among the waves are woven pink peonies, emblems of riches and honour. c. 1870.*

XIAPI : WOMAN'S CEREMONIAL COURT VEST

The *xiapi* was a long open waistcoat, attached at the sides with ribbons and decorated with dragons above a *lishui* wave border. These vests were usually embellished with a rank badge and sometimes their design incorporated the nine rank birds.

This rare xiapi has no rank badge, but all
nine rank birds are shown in the surrounding sky. c. 1850.

Sleevebands

Sleevebands, the most important of the trimmings on the robe, were often characterized by extremely delicate, detailed embroidery. One or two sets of sleevebands could be sewn on the outside of the sleeve. These smaller items often came from an embroidery studio that specialized in accessories. A tailor, visiting a client about to choose a new set of robes, would have brought along a sample book of trimmings, sleevebands and collars. Sometimes an additional set of sleevebands was sewn into the inside of the sleeves, so they could be seen when the sleeves were folded back. Every conceivable colour, design and material was used, often contrasting with the design of the garment itself.

A collection of exquisitely embroidered 19th-century sleevebands.

Mandarin ducks
faithfulness and marital happiness

Butterfly
longevity, summer, marital happiness and beauty

Bat
happiness

Prunus
first month, winter, perseverance and purity

Bat with peaches
'may you live long and be happy'

Peony
sixth month, spring, wealth and advancement

Bat with swastika
'may you have the greatest joy'

Lotus
seventh month, summer, purity and nobility

Pine tree
longevity, majesty and wisdom

Peaches
longevity

Chrysanthemum
tenth month, autumn, reclusiveness, gentility, fellowship, nobility and longevity

'Buddha's hand' citron
happiness and longevity

Orchid
eleventh month, charm in seclusion, friendship and nobility

Pomegranate
fertility in one's offspring, sons and a long lineage

The Three Plenties
a combination of peaches, 'Buddha's hand' citron and pomegranate

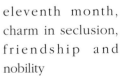

Narcissus
twelfth month, good fortune, purity, cleanliness and prosperity.

A CHRONOLOGY OF PERIODS IN CHINESE HISTORY

Palaeolithic	*c.* 600,000–7000 BC
Neolithic	*c.* 7000–1600 BC
Shang	*c.* 1600–1027 BC
Western Zhou	1027–771 BC
Eastern Zhou	770–256 BC
Spring and Autumn Annals	770–476 BC
Warring States	475–221 BC
Qin	221–206 BC
Western (Former) Han	206 BC–AD 8
Xin	9–24
Eastern (Later) Han	25–220
Three Kingdoms	220–265
Western Jin	265–316
Northern and Southern Dynasties	317–589
Sixteen Kingdoms	317–439
Former Zhao	304–329
Former Qin	351–383
Later Qin	384–417
Northern Wei	386–534
Western Wei	535–556
Northern Zhou	557–581
Sui	581–618
Tang	618–907
Five Dynasties	907–960
Liao	916–1125
Northern Song	960–1127
Southern Song	1127–1279
Jin (Jurchen)	1115–1234
Yuan (Mongol)	1279–1368
Ming	1368–1644
Qing (Manchu)	1644–1911
Republic of China	1911–1949
People's Republic of China	1949–

Bibliography

1. Cammann, Schuyler. *Costume in China 1644 to 1912*. Philadelphia Museum of Art Bulletin, No. 326, Vol 75, Fall 1979.

2. Chung, Young Y. *The Art of Oriental Embroidery: History, Aesthetics and Techniques*. Charles Scribner & Sons, New York, 1979.

3. Eberhard, Wolfram. *A Dictionary of Chinese Symbols*. Routledge & Kegan Paul, London, 1983.

4. Mailey, Jean. *Embroidery of Imperial China*. China Institute of America, New York, March 1978.

5. Priest, Alan. *Costumes from the Forbidden City*. The Metropolitan Museum of Art, New York, 1945.

6. Vollmer, John E. *In the Presence of the Dragon Throne*. Royal Ontario Museum, Toronto, 1977.

7. Vuilleumier, Bernard. *Symbolism of Chinese Imperial Ritual Robes*. The China Institute, London, 1939.

8. Williams, C.A.S. *Outlines of Chinese Symbolism & Art Motifs*. Dover Publications Inc, New York, 1976.

9. *Decoding Dragons*. University of Oregon Museum of Art, Eugene, 1983.

Teresa Coleman has lived in Hong Kong since 1982 and is a specialist in Chinese textiles. She studied painting at Wimbledon School of Art and later obtained a Master's degree in photography at London's Royal College of Art. Miss Coleman has collected textiles for many years and now owns an extensive collection of Chinese embroideries and costume accessories. Her readiness to share her expertise has helped contribute to the pleasant ambiance that has made her gallery so popular among both local collectors and visitors to Hong Kong.